Copyright ©2024 by Richard Jepson

ISBN: 9798322013709

All rights reserved.

No portion of this book may be reproduced in any form without written permission from the publisher or author, except as permitted by U.S. copyright law. This publication is designed to provide accurate and authoritative information in regard to the subject matter covered.

Neither the publisher nor the author shall be liable for any loss of profit or any other commercial damages, including but not limited to special, incidental, consequential, personal, or other damages.

1st Edition 2024

REFINING TO EXCELLENCE

A Busy Professional's Guide

to the Simple Principles of Lean Manufacturing

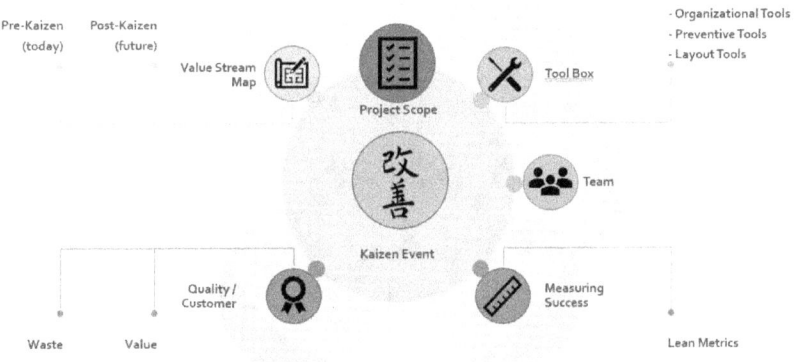

Table of Contents

Preface	1
Introduction - How To Use This Book	6
Defining Continuous Improvement and Lean Manufacturing	8
Lean Manufacturing Overview	13
The "Simplified" Story of Lean Manufacturing	14
The Visual Overview of What The Lean Approach Is	15
How to Be Successful with Lean:	18
Warning: Don't Be A Lean Zombie	18
Overview Worksheet	20
Step One: Project Scope	23
Action Items for Step One:	25
Step One Worksheet	26
Step Two: Form A Team	29
Action Items for Step Two:	32
Step Two Worksheet	33
Step Three: Understanding Your Customer	36
Defining Value Versus Waste Summary	37
The Seven Wastes of Lean	40
Value Added - Or What The Customer Asked For	44
Action Items for Step Three:	48
Step Three Worksheet	49

Step Four: Value Stream Mapping — **52**
    Action Items for Step Four: — 57
    Step Four Worksheet — 59

Step Five: Metrics — **62**
    Lean Metrics - Most Common — 68
    Action Items for Step Five: — 70
    Step Five Worksheet — 72

Step Six: Lean Tools — **75**
    5S - Lean's Organizational Tool — 76
    Lean's Visual Management Tool — 92
    Poka Yoke - Lean's Mistake Proofing Tool — 99
    Kanban - Lean's Inventory Tool — 108
    OEE - Lean's Productivity Tool — 114
    Lean's Root Cause Analysis Tools — 121

Step Seven: Kaizen Event — **132**
    Action Items for Step Seven: — 140
    Step Seven Worksheet — 142

Conclusion — **144**

Author Biography — **151**

Preface

Imagine a company enthusiastic about implementing Lean Manufacturing principles. They've read all the books, watched all the TED Talks, and are ready to streamline their processes like a well-oiled machine. But as they dive into their Lean journey, they encounter some unexpected hurdles that turn their well-intentioned efforts into comedy gold.

Meet Bob, the over-enthusiastic Lean champion. Armed with his trusty whiteboard and a stack of Post-it notes, he's ready to revolutionize the production line. He starts by implementing 5S methodology – Sort, Set in Order, Shine, Standardize, and Sustain. However, things take an interesting turn when he accidentally sorts away half of the office supplies, leaving the team scrambling for pens and sticky notes like squirrels gathering nuts for winter.

Then there's Karen, the efficiency guru. She decides to tackle the issue of wasted time by introducing a Lean inventory management. But her well-laid plans come crashing down when the delivery truck carrying crucial parts gets stuck in traffic, leaving the production line at a standstill. Now, instead of lean manufacturing, they're practicing the art of synchronized desk drumming while they wait.

Meanwhile, the CEO, inspired by success stories of Lean transformations, decides to cut costs by implementing Kanban systems everywhere. But instead of improving workflow, the office turns into a confusing maze of colored cards, and meetings devolve into debates over whether the blue card means "in progress" or "waiting for Bob to find the missing stapler."

As the weeks pass, it becomes increasingly clear that Lean Manufacturing isn't a silver bullet but more like a tricky jigsaw puzzle missing a few pieces.

The once-enthusiastic team finds themselves tangled in a web of well-meaning initiatives gone awry, with Bob sheepishly admitting that maybe they should've started with a smaller whiteboard.

In the end, the company learns that while Lean Manufacturing principles can lead to efficiency gains, they're not immune to Murphy's Law – anything that can go wrong will go wrong, especially when you least expect it, including the occasional office-wide scavenger hunt for the missing stapler.

So why do continuous improvement programs fail?

I believe there are two reasons:

- Lack of understanding of the tools and system
- Impatience of the process - jumping to the solution

Organizations attempt to implement improvement systems but are often too impatient. Leadership wants results without the effort of understanding the tools properly and for what the tools were designed to do. This "results first, process later" leads to the eventual failure of the system and the discouragement of the staff to continue on the continuous improvement journey.

You can see that in the following survey from APQC, where establishing a culture of continuous improvement is the top challenge.

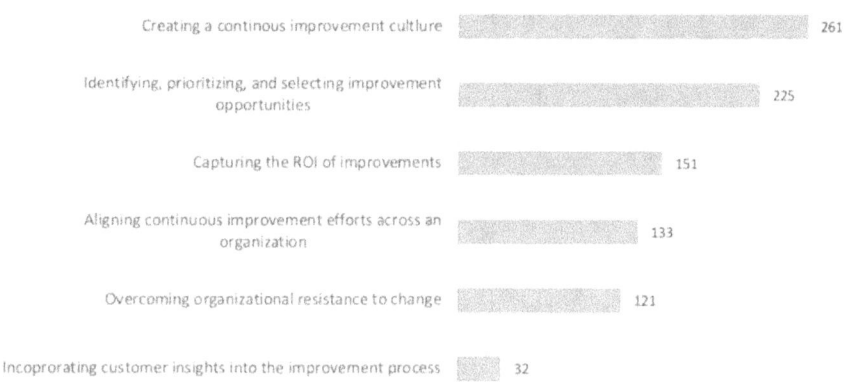

When an organization struggles to understand the basics of why they are doing an improvement program, there is never sufficient time to cultivate the behaviors to sustain the actions and mental energy to continue moving forward with the program.

This book is an attempt to simplify Lean Manufacturing down into bite-sized pieces that can be digested easily and understood quickly. With a solid understanding, the behaviors needed to form a continuous improvement culture are present and the system can organically grow with the organization.

Lean Manufacturing is a wonderful improvement system that can drastically refine an environment into excellence... not one of confusion and searching for lost staplers.

Welcome to refining to excellence!

Introduction - How To Use This Book

Continuous improvement can be an overwhelming endeavor. This pain point is why I wrote this book... to just focus on the most important principles of Lean Manufacturing and not everything ever created for Lean systems. By focusing on the 40% of Lean that gives you 90% of the return, the process is simplified to a manageable dose. Biggest bang for your buck!

So, how should you use this book?

Refining To Excellence has a *Seven Step* process of doing a Lean Manufacturing project. If you follow these steps, whether the project is big or small, you will see benefits to your products and processes. You will have successfully performed a Lean Project.

The book is organized so that each step has a principle to focus on, the foundational information to understand the principle, an action item list at the chapter's end to assist with execution, and checklist and note pages for your specific project.

Going step by step, as a new or novice Lean practitioner, is recommended in order to create a mental connection between tools, principles, and timing. Making this connection is important so that you begin thinking in a "Lean" manner and this is your ultimate end goal.

If you already have a basic fundamental understanding of Lean, you may find it more beneficial to jump around from principle to principle to assist for the specific portion of a Lean project you want to focus on. This technique is perfectly acceptable and is encouraged for simple projects.

Whatever you end up pursuing, it is my wish that you can stand up at the end of your Lean project in awe of the wonderful improvements that you have successfully completed. This is the best feeling in the whole world as a change agent. May you have an abundance of these feelings throughout your Lean journey.

Richard

Defining Continuous Improvement and Lean Manufacturing

Often I start training sessions with a simple question: "What is Lean Manufacturing?" or "What is Continuous Improvement?"

You would think that most students would have some sort of answer to these questions. To be fair, many have a good guess and are in the "ballpark." However, many are just confused because "lean" could mean different things. "Continuous Improvement" makes a bit more sense but it's so general in nature that it is hard to define what you are actually going to do.

Besides the names chosen for these programs, what also confuses students is the misconception of what the goal is.

With so many companies trying to implement a continuous improvement system for promotional purposes or to simply prove they have accomplished something, the front line employees are the first to become stuck in the mud of conflicting objectives. In an effort to do something, situations get worse. Instead of making a system of improvement, it becomes a system of metrics that drive the wrong behavior.

Correcting this objective confusion and avoiding the traps of management implementation are the reasons I decided to write this book.

The process needs simplification not expansion. The goals of training need to be clear and focused, not ambiguous and short sighted.

The objective of continuous improvement training is to transform the student's mentality into another state of understanding... one where they cannot see a situation the way they always have in the past because the understanding they have now received has been so "enlightening" that they are forced to recognize the situation with new improved eyesight.

When the light bulb over your head goes on from clarity of thought and understanding, you can never look back.

So... enough babbling, you are all wanting to know what is the definition of Lean Manufacturing, right? I'll keep it simple.

Lean Manufacturing is a program for understanding and improving the flow of a product or service thereby saving time and money.

A simple definition, do you agree?

So where in the world does the word "Lean" come into play you ask? Well, you are "leaning" out the waste, the stuff that is not valued, and reorganizing the process into the most efficient flow possible, for a price that a customer is willing to pay. However, we're getting ahead of ourselves again so I will refrain from digging the hole deeper.

Probably the most important thing to understand here is that even though these are programs, or a collection of tools to be used, this is not how we should view them. The most important takeaway is that these are philosophies of how to do things properly.

When we teach new professionals that we have a "system" or a "collection of tools" to implement, the usual outcome is not what is desired. Sometimes the outcome is so bad that the Lean program is abandoned or blamed for poor financial or performance results. There is only one word for this result:

Failure.

It reminds me of the old phrase that if all you have is a hammer, then everything around you becomes a nail. Giving someone just a system/tool (our hammer) and no "why" (or the theory) creates a room full of holes in the wall and the furniture destroyed.

When there's meaning behind WHY we do things and in what scenario we should use the tool, life changes and things get better.

As we go through this, the goal is to develop experience and deep understanding, so that when you get a similar problem or opportunity in the future, you will be able to say "I have seen this before" and understand what process steps and which tools to use for the improvement.

The goal is to make you better at how YOU problem solve.

When you get better at doing problem solving, everyone else wants to be around you because they know you can make a difference and make something better than it was previously.

Be better, faster, smarter. This opens doors.

Hopefully, it will be fun along the way too.

Let's get started.

Lean Manufacturing Overview

Lean manufacturing has been in my blood for over 20 years. It all started when I was a lonely manufacturing supervisor for a major medical device company. At the time, you could have called it magic and I would have believed you... because it was magic to me.

My first exposure was within about 5 months of being hired. I had an industrial engineer come to me asking to "streamline" my manufacturing lines. I didn't know what the heck he wanted to do to my product line and equipment. I looked at my boss, he shook his head that everything was okay, and I agreed to participate in something called a "Kaizen event."

My life changed that day.

Years later, I found myself in a Japanese manufacturing plant, transferring technology to our facility back in the States. What I saw in Japan transformed my mentality on how to implement Lean Manufacturing for the rest of my life because of the culture that I witnessed.

Both of these events formed my Simplified Lean Approach and what we will be discussing the rest of this book. It was a streamlined effort to understand and use the tools in the most effective and efficient way possible.

Let's start with the Lean Story though.

The "Simplified" Story of Lean Manufacturing

Lean manufacturing, or should we say the understanding and improvement of product flow, has been around for hundreds of years.

Although there are instances of rigorous process thinking in manufacturing all the way back to the Arsenal in Venice in the 1450s, the first person to truly integrate an entire production process was Henry Ford. At Highland Park, MI, in 1913 he married consistently interchangeable parts with standard work and moving conveyance to create what he called flow production.

As Kiichiro Toyoda, Taiichi Ohno, and others at Toyota looked at this situation in the 1930s, and more intensely just after World War II (when variety was increased and complicated the production flow), it occurred to them that a series of simple innovations might make it more possible to provide both continuity in process flow and a wide variety in product offerings. They therefore revisited Ford's original thinking, and invented the Toyota Production System.

Today, Lean is used in every industry and in every arena.

The Visual Overview of What The Lean Approach Is

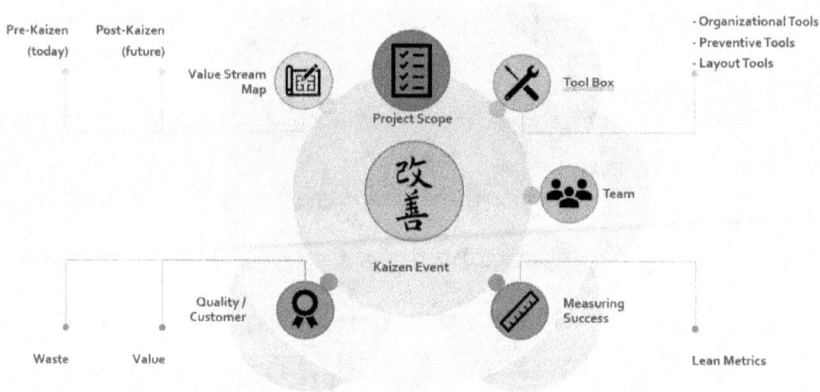

The above picture is your basic Lean Manufacturing diagram. With any improvement, you will have a process structure for organizing the appropriate actions to accomplish the improvement.

When this process analyzes the flow of product from point A to point B and creates the most efficient and effective way possible, that is called Lean Manufacturing.

So, with any project, you need a project scope. This is **Step One** of the Lean journey. The scope will focus on the area of interest and the magnitude of what is needed. This scope should be something that the business believes will be a significant help to bottom line results. If it is not significant, seriously question why you are working on it.

The project team is assembled next, **Step Two**, as you now know who needs to be involved in planning, executing, and closing the project out based on the scope. This team will be directly and indirectly involving members who can contribute in direct accomplishments of tasks or indirectly with support data or experience to help make decisions.

Step Three is understanding who the Customer is and what they consider to be Value or Waste. Lacking this insight could allow energy sucking action items to kill a good project.

Step Four is doing a Value Stream Map of the current and future states, thus giving you Opportunity Bursts on what to focus on.

Step Five is understanding what measurements are necessary (what metrics define success) so that as you execute the project, you will understand if you are winning or losing.

Step Six is deciding which other Lean tools will be necessary to the improvement activities. You rarely will use every lean tool available, so understanding the highest opportunities will drive which tools should be used.

Once all the surrounding areas of the above graphic are satisfied, you are now ready for **Step Seven**, the planning and executing of the Kaizen event (the central part of Lean Manufacturing).

Each of these steps will require additional explanations in separate sections but it is important for now just to understand that there is a basic order of progression through the Lean Manufacturing process.

As a point of warning, if the project is so simple of an improvement that you only need to use one Lean tool to be successful, don't be foolish enough to utilize the complete Lean Manufacturing sequence. Please, just do the Lean exercise or improvement and move on with life.

That would be the Lean thing to do.

How to Be Successful with Lean:

There are basic needs that are required to be successful with the Lean approach. It is very simple in concept but often difficult to execute well. They are:

- It takes effort and discipline
- It takes consistency
- It takes pride and passion
- It takes professionalism
- It takes everyone to get involved in maintaining the momentum

Take out one of these areas and you have a risk of not being successful with whatever Lean project you are trying to accomplish.

Warning: Don't Be A Lean Zombie

While working on a project early on in my career, there was a Lean Team coming down from corporate to "Lean Out" a process step that they felt was a serious bottleneck. All of us on the team thought it was a good idea to evaluate ways of improving the throughput.

However, the first thing we noticed with these Lean experts was that they didn't consult with the current engineering team about the process. This corporate team went about their business, decided what the issue was, and qualified the process with the updated process flow.

Sounds fine, right? Don't we all want streamlined processes and improved throughput? Of course we do… but…

It was a disaster.

The process that the team "leaned-out" was a batch process, one that required specific steps to be performed in an exact process order, so that the chemicals reacted in the preferred way. Since this team did not include the local engineering team (and their knowledge base) to make decisions on what was critical and what was trivial, they tampered with a process order that should have been left alone.

The result was going from a process that had 98% yields (and took 3 hours to complete) to a process that now had 60% yields (and took 2 hours to complete). What made matters even worse was that each failed batch was $30,000 worth of product - and we made the failed batches faster.

Once corporate found this out, I don't ever recall seeing those engineers again at the manufacturing plant. I don't recall seeing any emails from them ever again either. Hmmm, I wonder what happened to them?

What I learned from this experience was that you can't be a *Lean Zombie* - a person trained in Lean but meandering aimlessly around causing havoc wherever they go because they don't *understand* Lean.

You could also say a Lean Zombie is someone who doesn't fully understand what it means to make a process better. They have a Lean tool ready and just need a project to hit it upside the head with to say they did something.

Lean Zombies are bad news for your company, business, project teams, and yourself and you should avoid them at all costs, less you get bit by one and become one yourself.

Overview Worksheet

Checklist and Tasks

- ☐ _____
- ☐ _____
- ☐ _____
- ☐ _____
- ☐ _____
- ☐ _____
- ☐ _____
- ☐ _____
- ☐ _____
- ☐ _____
- ☐ _____

Notes

- _____
- _____
- _____
- _____
- _____
- _____
- _____
- _____
- _____
- _____
- _____

Step One: Project Scope

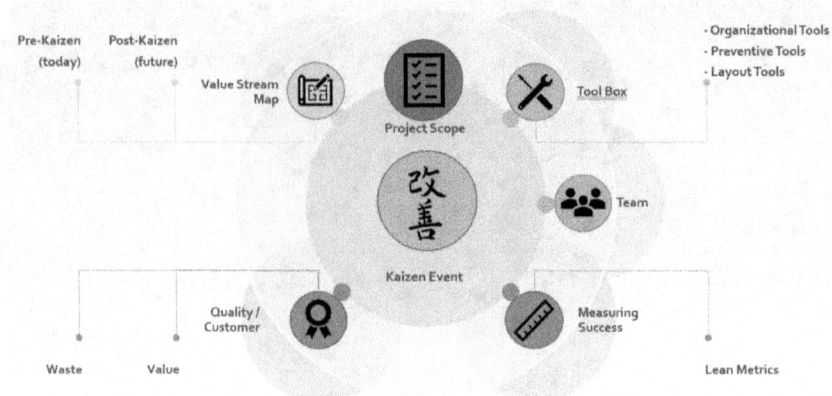

Okay, let's get going.

There are always areas that need improvement, you simply just need to understand which area or product line or project needs the help the most. You can decide this based on current or future needs but you should do something that matters to more than just you.

The scope should be focused on the current needs or issues that give the most return of effort applied.

The scope should define the department / production line / or group that will be the target of the Kaizen event and the outcome that is anticipated or needed.

The scope should also be large enough that it takes a few days to accomplish but not so long that you can't get it completed and tied up within a week's time frame. You want to get in, improve, and get out.

It is important to also understand that a scope can be reduced or expanded based on the need to simplify or compliment the activities needed to accomplish the goal of the event. One could say, "what is the maximum benefit the organization can achieve during the time allotment that has been given to the team?" Once you figure out this statement, the scope falls into place.

Action Items for Step One:

- Find the product line, area, or process that needs to be improved the most.
- Determine what the desired outcome looks like. What is the result?
- Establish boundaries to limit scope expansion.
- Review the scope with leadership and get approval to move forward.
- Document the scope into a concise statement that is easy to understand, communicate, and follow.

Step One Worksheet

Project Scope Checklist and Tasks

- [ ] _____
- [ ] _____
- [ ] _____
- [ ] _____
- [ ] _____
- [ ] _____
- [ ] _____
- [ ] _____
- [ ] _____
- [ ] _____
- [ ] _____
- [ ] _____
- [ ] _____
- [ ] _____
- [ ] _____
- [ ] _____
- [ ] _____
- [ ] _____
- [ ] _____
- [ ] _____
- [ ] _____

Notes

- _____
- _____
- _____
- _____
- _____
- _____
- _____
- _____
- _____
- _____
- _____
- _____
- _____
- _____
- _____
- _____
- _____
- _____
- _____
- _____
- _____
- _____
- _____
- _____

Step Two: Form A Team

Once you have decided which project to do, you need to organize a cross-functional team to attack the scope of your project. Forming a team is one of the integral parts of the Lean process inner circle (refer to the Lean Manufacturing diagram) and often becomes a second thought to those that work in Lean projects. Not putting effort into a proper team can be a critical error that can easily derail a potentially good project.

So, let's work on it.

What is your team? It shouldn't be too large (bureaucracy is a slow, painful death) and shouldn't be too small (need someone to help you survive).

I usually like seeing a team of 4 to 6 people. A team of one to two people (the core team) who are driving the project with two to four people from other departments that are supporting the project fits this structure.

The core team will be doing the heavy lifting and accomplishing most of the action items and will be responsible for the success of the project.

The supporting individuals should contribute with details and data that you will need to make the best decisions for the project.

Often you will need to pull the same leadership that approved the project scope into also approving the team members. Sometimes, the leadership has to make the project a priority to the supporting staff so that they don't completely blow your requests off.

Once the team is formed, the best thing you could do to be successful is to have a "who is responsible for what" meeting. Making sure everyone understands what is required of them saves a lot of anxiety later in the project.

There also may be a need to schedule a weekly or daily meeting to make sure the project moves forward on time and get results. Just make sure the meeting is truly needed as adding bureaucracy to any project is basically Anti-Lean. If the action isn't adding value to the company or customer, don't do it.

Action Items for Step Two:

The following are rules-of-thumb and should be molded to the size of your group, team, or company. The important thing to remember in this step is the formation of a team and subsequent delegation of tasks. Everything else is supportive to this goal.

- Determine the necessary skills relevant to the project scope.
- Select core team members (2 to 3).
- Select supporting team members (2 to 3).
- Establish expectations and responsibilities.
- Develop a list of needed resources.
- Establish a method of monitoring progress.

Step Two Worksheet

Project Team Checklist and Tasks

- ☐ _____
- ☐ _____
- ☐ _____
- ☐ _____
- ☐ _____
- ☐ _____
- ☐ _____
- ☐ _____
- ☐ _____
- ☐ _____
- ☐ _____
- ☐ _____
- ☐ _____
- ☐ _____
- ☐ _____
- ☐ _____
- ☐ _____
- ☐ _____
- ☐ _____
- ☐ _____
- ☐ _____
- ☐ _____

Notes

- _____
- _____
- _____
- _____
- _____
- _____
- _____
- _____
- _____
- _____
- _____
- _____
- _____
- _____
- _____
- _____
- _____
- _____
- _____
- _____
- _____
- _____
- _____
- _____
- _____

Step Three: Understanding Your Customer

In Lean Manufacturing, a customer is defined as the recipient of the product or service being produced. This definition extends beyond the end-user to include anyone who receives or interacts with the output of a process, whether internal or external to the organization.

In Lean principles, understanding and meeting customer needs and expectations are fundamental. This includes:

External Customers: These are the end-users or purchasers of the product or service. Understanding their needs, preferences, and expectations is crucial for delivering value and maintaining competitiveness.

Internal Customers: Within the organization, different departments or processes often rely on each other's output.

Each department or process is considered an internal customer of the preceding one. For example, in a manufacturing setting, the assembly line is the customer of the fabrication department.

Understanding customer requirements helps eliminate waste, streamline processes, and improve overall quality.

Lean Manufacturing emphasizes delivering value (or Value Added) to customers by focusing on what they truly need and eliminating activities that do not contribute to that value (or Waste).

Defining Value Versus Waste Summary

Value and Waste, in the Lean World, are the opposite sides of the same coin. Both are defined by starting with what is important to the Customer.

With this in mind, *Value* is anything that either creates the product, makes the product better, and/or transforms it in some way that the customer is willing to pay for it. *Waste* is basically anything that isn't Value. There are seven types of Wastes and they will be discussed later on.

The most important part of understanding Value is by trying to understand what the customer truly cares about in relation to the product you are providing. ***Cost***, ***On-time Delivery***, and ***Quality*** are the typical driving factors of what the customer is concerned about.

Reduction of cost is a win for the customer.

Delivering the product on time or better, in the quantity required, is another win for the customer.

Maintaining or surpassing the quality requirements of the product rounds out the customer needs and is yet another win.

Any slippage of expectations on these three categories (or specifications), could easily impact your business. We call these *customer specifications* so that we can monitor and measure how the Lean process is compliant to the minimal level of that specification.

Any effort that improves these specifications is "Value Added," and anything that takes away from that is "Wasted Effort." You will hear these used often among Lean Zombies, but they rarely understand what the true meaning is.

The Japanese are more broad when they discuss waste. There are actually three ways of discussing waste in Japanese: Muda, Mura, and Muri. *Muda* (無駄) is defined as futility, uselessness, idleness, superfluity, waste, wastefulness. *Mura* is unevenness and *Muri* is overburden.

When we say "Waste" in English, it usually is thought of being something thrown in the garbage or a defect. When you look at how the Japanese look at waste, you can see it incorporates a laundry list of other categories. These categories don't help with improving the flow of products, so it makes perfect sense to include it into the definition of waste. Idle time or unevenness will slow a process down and therefore is a natural area for improvement.

So it is important here to understand what is Waste and what is Value in more detail, in order to organize the activities you must focus on for elimination or improvement.

Let's start with defining waste in terms of Lean Manufacturing. We call them the "Seven Sins" of continuous improvement.

The Seven Wastes of Lean

With that said, let me introduce you to TIMWOOD. He's a guy you don't want to have around. TIMWOOD is an acronym for the Seven Wastes of Lean. They are:

- Transportation
- Inventory
- Motion
- Waiting
- Overproduction
- Over-processing
- Defects

Transportation refers to the effort of relocation of finished or in process products that could lead to deterioration, misplacement, longer lead times and additional workloads. The more effort you send transporting things, the more expense you absorb as a business.

Inventory refers to storage, whether short or long term, of raw materials, WIP, or finished goods. Inventories should be minimized based on lead time, process time, and customer demand and not based on idleness, laziness, or mismanagement. Storage costs money in materials (cash not being used immediately to support customer needs), labor (cash used in moving and accounting for materials), and overhead (racks, building, and utilities all cost money and add to overall product cost).

Motion refers to useless or unnecessary relocation of people and equipment during the manufacturing process that could impact timeliness of product flow. This waste could also refer to pointless activities or motions in the processing of the product that could be performed in a more concise or purposeful manner.

Waiting refers to the time lost due to materials, equipment, or people not being available but needed to perform a process. This waste loses valuable time that could be used in a productive manner. Waiting can be one of the most expensive issues in a process yet one of the easiest wastes to overcome.

Overproduction refers to the production of finished goods or services above and beyond what the customer has requested or the market needs. Using valuable resources, and money, to make a product that sits in a warehouse, slowly dying on a shelf, is a failure of operational planning and organizational strategy.

Over-processing refers to activities (such as over inspection, overly complicated work instructions, or pointless tasks) that do not create value for the customer. This waste burdens the production system and distracts from what should be done and not be done. Spending money on activities that the customer didn't ask for or doesn't care about is a sin in the Lean universe.

Defects refers to any rejected finished good or subassembly that is classified as defective by the customer's requirements. This waste is created by misaligned work instructions, failure of equipment, or poor execution. Defects become more expensive the farther down the assembly process they get detected. Money spent on labor and materials for products sitting in the trash can is painful for everyone.

That's all seven of the wastes that we try to avoid in Lean systems. Understanding these "Sins" of Lean are essential to understanding how to streamline any process. Eliminating them is our constant battle. Preventing them is our daily goal. Living without is our end goal.

When someone truly internalizes the elimination of waste from a system and it becomes second nature to them, how you look at processes or how you understand the flow of product will never be the same.

Another simple way of looking at waste is by categorizing them into **People**, **Process**, or **Product**. In the figure here, you see which wastes are caused by which category.

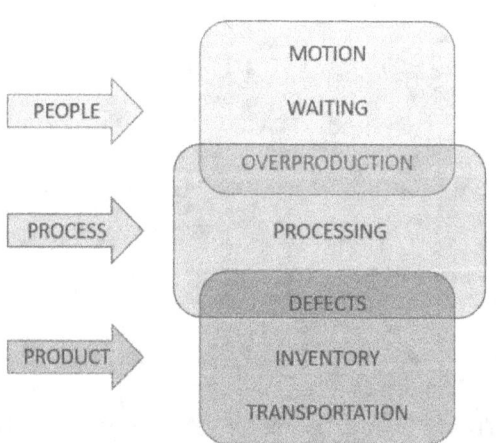

This perspective can be quite helpful to minimize or eliminate the waste from the product flow by understanding who or what is causing it.

For example, if a product is waiting between process steps, that is usually a People problem. If there are too many defects, it could be a Process or Product problem.

Of course, you could argue that everything can be a people problem or a process problem or even a product problem, but this is a general categorization on what influences potentially could cause the specific waste being analyzed.

Value Added - Or What The Customer Asked For

Value, as we defined before, is satisfying what the Customer asked for in cost, delivery, and quality. Anything that "adds" to this "value" is therefore "Value-Added." Anything that doesn't add value can be considered waste. Makes sense, right? So, let's dig deeper into the concept of Value-Added.

If we start with the customer in mind, we think about what is most important about the product. Once again, the customer wants a quality product, on time, for a fair price. If we break these characteristics or specifications down one more level to what the customer wants, you might see them described as such:

The Customer wants this for "Quality" -

- Product **must** be able to have tensile strength of 3 lbf
- Product **must** be purple colored
- Product **must** be <<insert any critical physical attribute>>

The Customer wants this for "On Time Delivery" -

- Once ordered, product **must** arrive within 30 days from confirmation
- Product **must** be shipped standard ground to save on expenses
- All product **must** be <<insert critical delivery need>>

The Customer wants this for "Cost / Price" -

- Product **must** be less than $10 for standard version
- Product **must** be less than $25 for all custom versions
- Product **must** be <<insert critical costing need>>

One can quickly see that each specification is a "Must" and therefore critical to the customer.

One can then quickly understand that each specification brings value to the customer because it is a critical must.

Without the specification being satisfied, the expectation of the customer is not met and the result is probably the product being returned for exchange or refund. A canceled order is twice as burdensome as any issue in trying to fulfill a customer's need.

Value-Added is now easier to see in the detail of specifications because you can measure if you are winning or losing. A clever person can also Lean out the manufacturing process to make sure these critical specs are met by additional measurements earlier and throughout the process to verify you will deliver that value.

The measurement process cascades throughout the Value Stream Map and gives those involved the data necessary to make proper decisions.

Understanding the Value Stream (the process flow) and where Value exists and Waste lives becomes the next most important step and that is the next topic.

Action Items for Step Three:

To better understand your customer, you may use the following action items. Some action items may be more effective than others. It is important to understand what the customer considers Value and Waste. However you feel you can do this, go for it.

- Define your target audience / customer.
- Use surveys, interviews, and focus groups to gather insights about your customer.
- Study market trends and competitors that affect your customer.
- Include customer demographic details, interests, pain points, and goals.
- Encourage reviews and testimonials to gain insights into customer experiences.
- Regularly solicit feedback through surveys, feedback forms, and post-purchase emails.
- Actively listen to customer suggestions and complaints.
- Document feedback into measurable specifications that can be monitored and recorded for process / product adjustment.

Step Three Worksheet

Customer Checklist and Tasks

- ☐ _____
- ☐ _____
- ☐ _____
- ☐ _____
- ☐ _____
- ☐ _____
- ☐ _____
- ☐ _____
- ☐ _____
- ☐ _____
- ☐ _____
- ☐ _____
- ☐ _____
- ☐ _____
- ☐ _____
- ☐ _____
- ☐ _____
- ☐ _____
- ☐ _____
- ☐ _____
- ☐ _____
- ☐ _____

Notes

- _____
- _____
- _____
- _____
- _____
- _____
- _____
- _____
- _____
- _____
- _____
- _____
- _____
- _____
- _____
- _____
- _____
- _____
- _____
- _____
- _____
- _____
- _____
- _____

Step Four: Value Stream Mapping

You have your scope, your team, your customer's needs, and you are ready to make something good happen. Before you run outta the room like Scoobie Doo, you need to avoid the trap of jumping straight into what you "believe" to be the most important tasks as opposed to what truly are the important tasks.

We make a lot of mistakes and waste a lot of time making decisions based on little to no data. Our "opinion" and "gut" can be correct but they should be validated first. This is where the Value Stream Map comes into play.

A Value Stream Map (VSM) is an overview of the scoped project on one piece of paper. It comes in two forms, a current state map and a future state map. The VSM looks at the "start of" to the "end of" the product flow, broken into bite-sized steps that are meaningful to the process.

Critical to this breakdown is the information that is collected at each process step. This information includes the cycle time (C/T), the change over time (C/O), and the uptime.

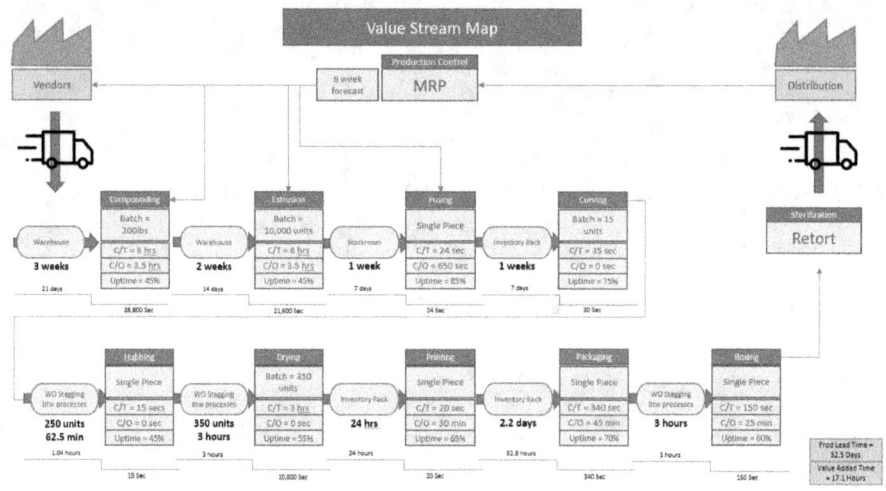

Let's look at the VSM step closer.

These process steps should be divided into manageable parts that represent the process flow but not so detailed that it confuses the ability to extract what to do with the information. The graph shows that each step is titled and the critical information cascades beneath it. Each step also shows the Work In Process (WIP) or inventory that is directly in front of it and what is directly after it.

Finally, it places the process time on a lower "time bar" that is used to sum the total Production Lead Time (all process cycle times and waiting times) and the Value Added Time (just the process cycle times).

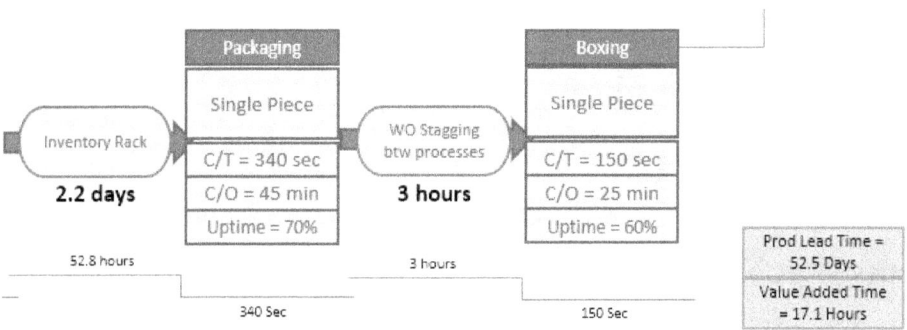

You can see from the example presented, that Value Added Time is a fraction of the Production Lead Time. This relationship will typically be seen because process flow in a business has lots of opportunity naturally in it. People love to put things on shelves. Workers like to work in their own world (batch processes) and not be in concert with another (one piece flow). Processes drift or become unbalanced. There are infinite possibilities of waste in a system.

Creating a Value Stream shows where the Value-Added steps are found and where the Waste of the system is found. Where we find areas to reduce the waste, or increase the value, in our VSM becomes our improvement opportunities or VSM

Bursts. Waste and Value will be defined in the next chapter so don't worry if these terms don't completely make sense.

Seeing an overview of a process adds detail that you just don't get from your gut or your quick opinion. This is why having a "current state" Value Stream Map is the third step of our Lean Manufacturing journey.

Once you have a current state version, you see your VSM bursts, you can then forecast what the future state version could be.

Take my word for it. Do your Value Stream Map and see what I am talking about. You'll thank me afterwards.

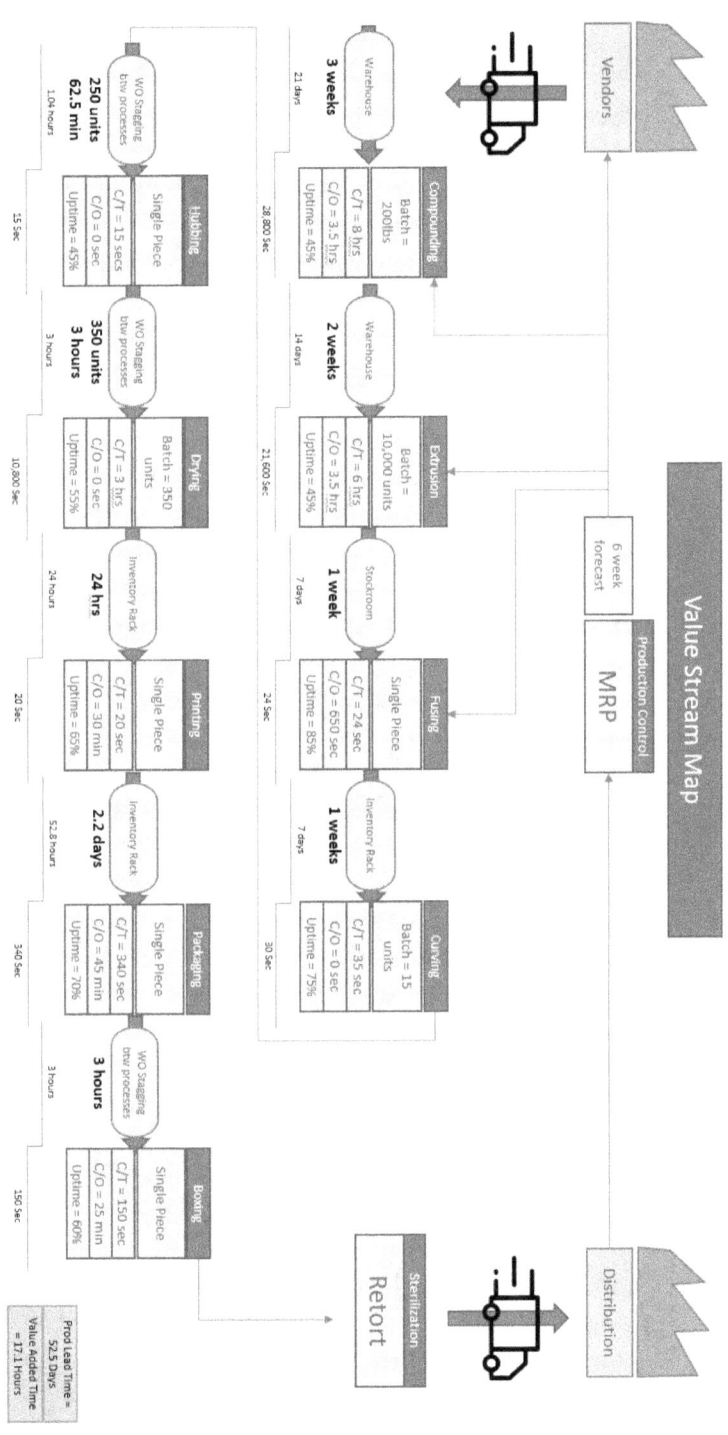

Action Items for Step Four:

- **Draw the Current State map**: Use symbols to represent each step in the process, including material flows, information flows, and decision points.
- Document process steps: Identify each step in the process, including any delays, rework loops, or handoffs between departments.
- Capture data: Record cycle times, lead times, inventory levels, and other relevant metrics at each step.
- Note inventory levels: Highlight inventory levels at each stage of the process to identify areas of waste or inefficiency.
- Include information flow: Map how information flows through the process, including communication between departments, systems used, and decision-making processes.

- **Analyze the Current State** by:
- Identify waste: Look for areas of waste such as waiting time, excess inventory, overproduction, unnecessary movement, defects, and unused employee skills.
- Calculate lead time: Determine the total lead time for the process from start to finish.

- Calculate cycle time: Determine the cycle time for each step in the process.
- Identify bottlenecks: Identify steps in the process where work accumulates or queues form, causing delays and inefficiencies.
- Brainstorm solutions: Engage the cross-functional team in brainstorming sessions to identify potential improvements to the process.
- Prioritize improvements: Evaluate potential improvements based on their impact on lead time, cycle time, cost, quality, and customer satisfaction.
- Develop an action plan: Create a plan for implementing the identified improvements, including timelines, responsible parties, and resource requirements.
- Design the ideal process: Use the insights gained from analyzing the current state to design a future state that eliminates waste, reduces lead time, and improves efficiency.

- **Draw the Future State map**: Create a new value stream map that represents the optimized process flow.
- Document changes: Highlight the differences between the current state and the future state, including process changes, resource reallocation, and performance improvements.

Step Four Worksheet

Value Stream Map Checklist and Tasks

☐ _____
☐ _____
☐ _____
☐ _____
☐ _____
☐ _____
☐ _____
☐ _____
☐ _____
☐ _____
☐ _____
☐ _____
☐ _____
☐ _____
☐ _____
☐ _____
☐ _____
☐ _____
☐ _____
☐ _____
☐ _____

Notes

- _____
- _____
- _____
- _____
- _____
- _____
- _____
- _____
- _____
- _____
- _____
- _____
- _____
- _____
- _____
- _____
- _____
- _____
- _____
- _____
- _____
- _____
- _____
- _____
- _____

Step Five: Metrics

Making decisions is a daily exercise. We make good decisions. We make bad decisions. Sometimes we even decide not to make decisions, which is really still making a decision.

What makes a person really good at making the correct decisions is how much data they have to navigate through the risks and challenges of what the outcome of that decision creates. Intuitively, the more data, the better the decisions. This is not always the case.

What we all need when making decisions is the most critical information that objectively spells out the advantages and disadvantages of the paths that are options. This information should give us clarity on making the next move.

When I find someone who is struggling in making a decision, I always tell them to get more information in the areas that they are having an issue. After they get this data, it is usually much clearer for them to finally choose a course of action.

The goal in getting information is therefore critically important in Lean Manufacturing as we want the most advantageous decisions to make the most beneficial improvements. This is where metrics come into play and what we crave more than anything is a good metric.

What makes a good metric? Glad you asked.

A Good Metric:
- Needs to actually be something we *care about* and *aligns* with business goals and strategies,
- Needs to be something that we *can influence* or take action as a result of, in a *timely manner*,
- Needs to be something we can *accurately quantify*,
- Needs to *minimize* secondary *"negative" responses*,
- Which will then help make *better decisions*.

As one can see, a good metric can be a bit complicated. It's complicated only because you have to make sure you are measuring and collecting data for the right reasons and can therefore further the business with the information you get. Each of the bolded/italicized statements create a circumstance where you can make better decisions.

Most of the bolded statements are self explanatory, but you probably are wondering why it is stated to minimize secondary negative responses. Pages and pages of examples could be shown of unanticipated negative responses to a perfectly good metric. We should therefore be careful of what we measure.

My favorite example of a good metric gone wrong is from a friend that worked at a call center where they were bonused based on how quickly they resolved the issue from the caller. Faster call times equal faster resolutions, which in turns equals more customers serviced. Right?

It is all fun and games until someone "games" the metric and gets bonused by hanging up on people. Faster call times equaled more bonuses but also equaled really ticked off customers.

Be aware of how a metric may cascade into complete chaos and end up destroying all Lean progress along the way. Beware of negative secondary responses.

Here is another situation that you should be aware of.

The average person loves to be right. In the heat of a battle, we use our gut instinct to guess what would be the right choice or the right decision. There is high risk in making gut instinct decisions unless we are well versed in the topic or environment the decision is based in.

Patience is therefore needed when making very important decisions. In new and novel situations, it is prudent to first understand what data you need to make the most informed decision, then go out and get it. Establishing metrics in these areas become the backbone of the Lean process.

It should be said though, in true Lean fashion, the longer a decision takes to make, the less Lean it becomes. Waiting is a Lean waste, is it not?

We mitigate this obstacle by always having the most important data available for future decisions. Maintaining metric trackers and visual management boards becomes second nature to making daily decisions. However, if the decision is minor, we don't worry so much about the risk of making a bad decision because the risk of a bad decision is minimal. Either way, the decision can be made quickly and the risk is usually low.

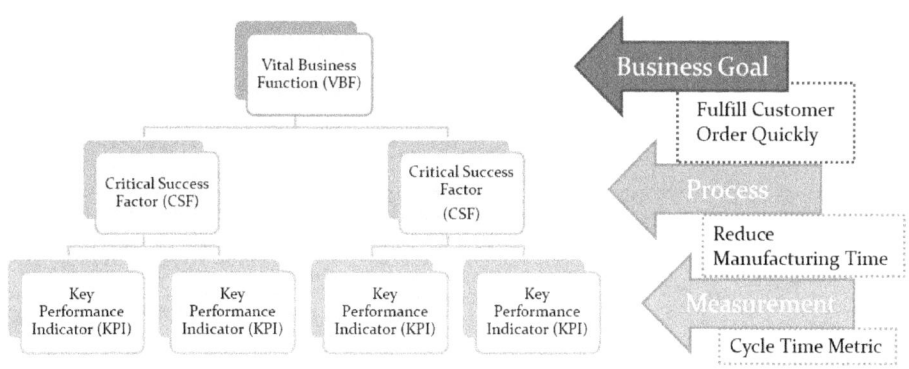

One last discussion point about Metrics can be visualized by the graph above. Vital business functions (VBF) are needs that live on top of all Lean metrics. These typically are company wide business goals that focus on the overall strategy of the company.

These VBF's are high level metrics that cascade down to critical success factors (CSF). CSF's reside lower in the organization, typically at the process steps, and support directly the VBF's of the company. CSF's are much more numerous and are created specifically because the VBf's are communicated.

At the base level, we find the key performance indicators (KPI) that measure the most important aspects of the floor for each CSF that is being monitored. When a KPI isn't measured or a reading falls outside the desired KPI window, everyone responsible for that KPI jumps into action.

Missing a KPI means that a CSF can be off, which potentially means a VBF will miss the business target for the company. Sounds like "Blah blah blah." Translation: If enough base metrics are missed, the company goals will eventually be missed. This is bad.

The take home message: Maintaining the metrics at the floor level becomes base business for anyone in a Lean Manufacturing company to succeed with top line goals and expectations.

Lean Metrics - Most Common

It may be easiest (and convenient) to simply list each major Lean metric below for reference, so here we go:

- Cycle Time - time it takes to start one part in a process till the next part is started in the same process.
- Takt Time - rate at which you need to produce a product to satisfy customer demand.
- Change Over Time - time required to transition a machine or process line from one product type to another product type.
- Line Balance - condition where all cycle times within a process are approximately the same time.
- OEE - also called Overall Equipment Effectiveness, is a ratio measurement of machine availability, quality, and performance.
- Throughput - is the average number of products produced over a unit of time.

- <u>Total Days of Inventory</u> - is a measurement of the required time to generate sales equivalent to the inventory value held.
- <u>Total Lead Time</u> - is the period of time needed from the very start of a process to the very end of a process, typically denoted from raw materials to shipped finished good units.

This list of metrics are the most common Lean Metrics used and can be found easily in any process. Each metric provides detail and data that should be useful in running any operation efficiently.

Your situation and business may need different metrics to run the process in the most effective way to guarantee what the customer needs most is what is completed. Therefore, make sure you establish "Good Metrics" and follow-up often to confirm you are getting the results desired.

Don't turn into my friend's call center.

Action Items for Step Five:

- Review your Value Stream Map and confirm that each process step is complete with the necessary Lean Metrics.
- Review your company's goals and expectations and compare your project to these metrics.
- Evaluate your Value Stream Map for the KPI's that affect your most important expected results of your project.
- Decide on how and what data will be collected, analyzed, and how any follow-up will be completed.
- Assess each potential metric based on its relevance, measurability, actionability, and alignment with your objectives. Consider whether the metric provides meaningful insights into your business performance and whether you can influence it.
- Prioritize the metrics based on their importance to your business objectives and their feasibility in terms of data availability and ease of measurement.
- Establish targets or benchmarks for each metric based on historical performance, industry standards, or best practices. These targets will help you track progress and identify areas for improvement.

- Confirm that the metrics will help satisfy customer requirements.

Step Five Worksheet

Metric Checklist and Tasks

- [ ] _____
- [ ] _____
- [ ] _____
- [ ] _____
- [ ] _____
- [ ] _____
- [ ] _____
- [ ] _____
- [ ] _____
- [ ] _____
- [ ] _____
- [ ] _____
- [ ] _____
- [ ] _____
- [ ] _____
- [ ] _____
- [ ] _____
- [ ] _____
- [ ] _____
- [ ] _____
- [ ] _____
- [ ] _____

Notes

Step Six: Lean Tools

Now that you have a Value Stream Map, have analyzed it for opportunities, and your metrics are established, you need a few Lean tools to help you improve value and minimize waste in your system or process.

The Lean tools presented are the most commonly used improvement methods and have specific areas where they are most effective. You may use or may not use these tools in your Lean journey but it is important that you are aware of them and what they are good at fixing.

5S - Lean's Organizational Tool

Teasing my wife is a pastime for me. Of course, teasing me is a pastime for her. For years, she would lose her phone or her keys. "Have you seen my keys? I seem to have misplaced them." I would often reply, "Interesting, that doesn't seem to be a problem for me." A smug look from her confirms that I should help her, not mock her.

Honestly though, why wasn't it a problem for me? That's because I had a system of where my phone or my keys were placed once I was done with them. When I needed them, I didn't have to use time and energy to remember where they were last placed - because I always put them back where they belonged.

Without a system, or process, life leans towards chaos.

5S comes to save the day for unorganized work areas. Of all the Lean tools, 5S can be your friend faster than another other tool.

Basically, 5S organizes shared spaces or spaces where there is a lot of tooling or equipment. Organizing the space can then reduce time and effort finding these tools or equipment when needed. Organization also prevents ordering tooling that you already have that may be hidden somewhere. Organization also prevents tooling from disappearing because it is not accounted for on a daily basis.

So, what is 5S?

5S stands for Seiri (整理), Seiton (整頓), Seisou (清掃), Seiketsu (清潔), and Shitsuke (躾). What, more Japanese? You're killing me Smalls! Properly translated into English, it would be Arrangement, Tidy, Cleaning, Cleanliness, and Discipline.

Of course, the acronym of ATCCD isn't as cool sounding as 5S. So in Lean terminology, it roughly is defined as Sort, Set, Shine, Standardize, and Sustain.

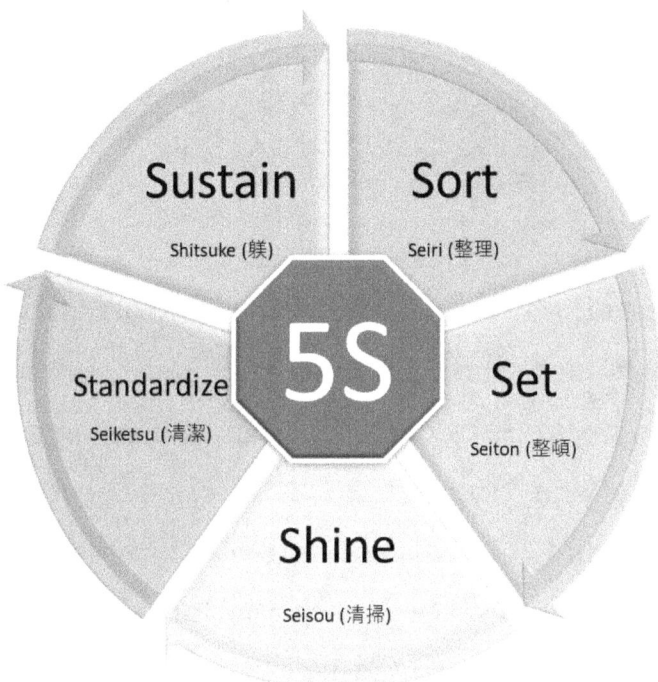

Before beginning the 5S cycle, the creation of a 5S team will help ensure the success of a 5S initiative. The team should include staff, frontline workers, and management. This organization confirms that core business areas are focused on, the right individuals are included, and the owners have a part in the process.

SORT

After the team is assembled, we start with **Sort**. The process begins by culling through everything in the target area, whether it be in manufacturing, an office, or a hospital environment, and *eliminating all unnecessary items*. Keep only the absolute essentials and store or throw away the rest. The entire team should be involved in the sorting process so an accepted, general consensus about what is and isn't necessary can be reached.

Defining what is necessary can be fairly straightforward. If an item is used daily, it is classified as necessary. If an item is used weekly, maybe it is necessary but it is placed in a "department" tooling area. If an item is used monthly, it should be classified as unnecessary and placed outside the general area in a "facility" related area. If an item hasn't been used for years, it is most definitely unnecessary and you should sell it or throw it away.

You will need to be brutal with the classification of necessary and unnecessary as the "hoarders" of the group will want everything kept or defined as necessary.

The necessary items are left in the area, the unnecessary items are placed away from the area in a temporary hold zone for elimination or retrieval.

Having buy-in from the team during the Sort phase is absolutely necessary as everyone will need to be onboard with the decisions or unnecessary items will return back faster than a bounced check.

SET

Set In Order: The next step is all about arranging the remaining items and creating an organized workspace. The straightening, labeling, etc. during this phase are all aimed at promoting an efficient workflow.

There are many valuable tools and procedures that can be implemented to make this stage a success. These include painting or labeling floors to indicate specific work areas, using tapes and labels to outline where tools or other supplies should go, special bins to store supplies and for inventory control, shelving and cabinets to solve storage issues, and more.

Set In Order is my favorite 5S step because it is the most creative part of the process. Defining locations, making shadow boards, arranging items in common categories, and labeling areas can be very visibly pleasing.

This step is also where you can minimize space needed and place the critical items closest to where they will be needed the most in the most efficient method possible.

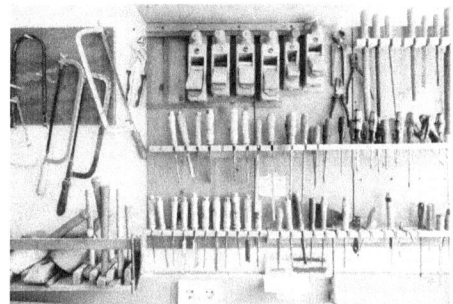

SHINE

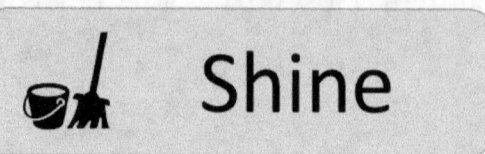

Shine: After the unnecessary items have been discarded, and the work area organized and made more efficient, then the cleaning process can begin. Sweeping, shining, and making the work area tidy helps workers to quickly recognize where leaks, broken parts, or malfunctions are located and get them repaired.

A nice side effect of Shine is improved safety measures that you can get credit for during this phase. When broken parts or cleanliness issues are addressed, a reduction of safety issues is a common outcome.

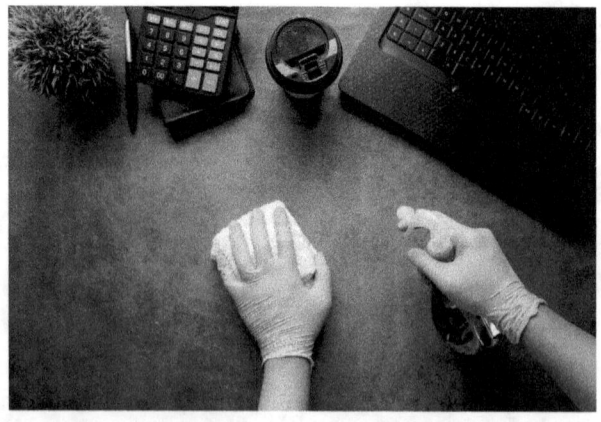

Once these first three steps of the 5S process are complete, evaluation of cleanliness needs to be practiced on a daily basis before, during, and after work is performed in this area. Workers need to make it a habit to clean the workplace in order to keep things from getting messy.

STANDARDIZE

Standardize: When the first three steps of the 5S process have been completed, attention needs to shift to creating a detailed procedure to standardize these practices. Because 5S is a visual process, some of the handy tools for this step include signs, checklists, charts, and scoreboards.

The Standardize step requires the most training and practice to promote the consistency needed for a successful 5S initiative. Preference on standardization is defined by the team or company, but it is important not to overcomplicate the proceduralization. Simple checklists are typically sufficient for this phase.

SUSTAIN

Sustain: Achieving success with the first four steps means nothing if the fifth step, Sustain, is overlooked. Maintaining the 5S process and creating good habits can be encouraged by visual reminders such as signs or posters around the work area. Regular meetings or routine walk throughs to review procedures and to discuss new issues will keep the focus on sustaining 5S efforts.

Recall that the Japanese refer to this step as "Discipline," and it takes discipline from all levels of the organization to maintain the benefits of a 5S project.

Closing Thoughts of the 5S Process:

"A bad system will defeat a good person every time," said W. Edwards Deming, a consultant of statistical control procedures for post-WWII Japan. Just because an organization implements a 5S/Lean program doesn't mean it's doing it for the right reasons or that it will lead to business successes.

Any Lean tool can be used improperly and for the wrong reasons. Lean tools can also be used indiscriminately and therefore not get the results that are expected.

One of my favorite "Lean-Gone-Wrong" stories was when I was working out in the Western States doing manufacturing engineering.

I went down to the production leader to discuss some issues that I needed her help with solving. Upon entering her office, I noticed that she had "5S'd" her desk.

There was outline tape around her mouse, her keyboard… around everything, including her coffee cup. With each outline tape came a small label stating what the object inside the outline should be.

What do you think I told her?

I asked "what in the world are you doing?" I explained that 5S'ing work stations is mainly intended for shared spaces, where tooling location and organization would help speed up the individual's performance.

My coworker's desk was not shared and did not have significant tooling that needed to be accounted for. The outlining and labeling of her computer keyboard, which was not going to move nor needed identification, was a waste of time and misuse of the Lean tools. She stared back at me confused and speechless.

My Coworker didn't understand the purpose of Lean. She was implementing Lean for the sake of implementing Lean, regardless of the outcome or the benefit.

All she had to do was clean her "crap" up.

When you use a Lean tool for the wrong reasons, the process dies slowly because it becomes the butt of jokes and water cooler criticism. Remember why you do something and what benefit it will serve. If it's a publicity stunt, it will backfire on you. If it is a meaningful project, everyone will see it and appreciate the effort and rewards.

All else fails, just use your Mom's advice to "Just clean your crap up!"

5S Worksheet

Checklist and Tasks

- [ ] _____
- [ ] _____
- [ ] _____
- [ ] _____
- [ ] _____
- [ ] _____
- [ ] _____
- [ ] _____
- [ ] _____
- [ ] _____
- [ ] _____
- [ ] _____
- [ ] _____
- [ ] _____
- [ ] _____
- [ ] _____
- [ ] _____
- [ ] _____
- [ ] _____
- [ ] _____
- [ ] _____

Notes

Lean's Visual Management Tool

I am a very visual person. I learn more efficiently by seeing things work or by seeing things displayed. So when Visual Management was first presented to me, it was very natural for me to implement it.

What is Visual Management you say?

Simply put, it is using visual displays to measure performance or translate information in a quick and concise manner. Whether it is scoreboards, production control charts, team communication boards, or other types of visible cues, visual management displays keep vital information flowing between management and employees, as well as between individuals, cells, and departments. They open communication and information sharing within the enterprise.

An easy example of visual management is a Visual Control Chart. A visual control chart is...

- any printed or hand-written chart that:
- is used for monitoring or controlling any aspect of a process,
- is posted in plain site very near the place where the actual work is done,
- is frequently updated with the latest results (timely enough to effectively respond to problems - not just historical post mortems),
- graphically highlights problems,
- has notes clearly articulating the reasons for "misses" (differences between expected vs. actual results),
- and can be understood by a newcomer standing 10 feet away.

Other examples of visual management are:

- **Kanban stations/cards** - tracks inventory levels (under / at / over) and generates action to refill inventory locations when needed.
- **5S boards** - monitoring and assessing the current status of a work area for cleanliness and organization, thus fulfilling the "Sustain" aspect of the 5S process.
- **Andon lights** - gives current status of equipment or process, and depending on the equipment used, can transmit downtime to those that need to know it.

- **Metric boards** - documents production or organizational goals and metrics to current production or departmental results.
- **Safety boards** - highlights daily results of injury, training, and projects and compares them to facility or company targets.

- **Floor / wall markings** - defines areas of danger, restricted access, production lines, and safety equipment so staff and guests will understand immediately what is expected or where things are located.

So why do we use Visual Management?

Another great question. Transparency supports identification and elimination of waste and ensures no problems are hidden. When you can quickly see what is going on, then you don't waste time and energy trying to find out what's happening. If you can see flow stoppers, you can take steps to remove them.

Simple signals let us know something needs attention. A red card on a piece of laboratory equipment means it requires maintenance, a green one confirms it is ready for use. A labeled but empty space on a bench indicates clearly what is missing.

Visual management, when performed consistently and clearly, will help an organization understand the key information relating to department or facility goals and if they are being reached. Visual management also helps to quickly resolve issues because attention is drawn to the problem based on being visible.

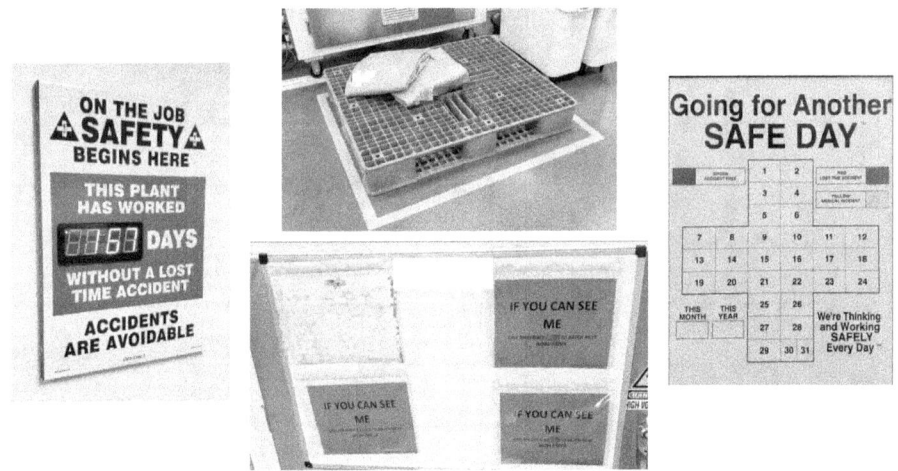

Visual Management Worksheet

Checklist and Tasks

- [ ] _____
- [ ] _____
- [ ] _____
- [ ] _____
- [ ] _____
- [ ] _____
- [ ] _____
- [ ] _____
- [ ] _____
- [ ] _____
- [ ] _____
- [ ] _____
- [ ] _____
- [ ] _____
- [ ] _____
- [ ] _____
- [ ] _____
- [ ] _____
- [ ] _____
- [ ] _____
- [ ] _____

Notes

Poka Yoke - Lean's Mistake Proofing Tool

Poka yoke (ポカヨケ) is a Japanese term that means "fail safing" or "mistake proofing" - literally "avoiding blunders."

The term Poka Yoke was applied by Shigeo Shingo in the 1960s to industrial processes designed to prevent human errors. Shingo redesigned a process in which factory workers, while assembling a small switch, would often forget to insert the required spring under one of the switch buttons.

In the redesigned process, the worker would perform the task in two steps, first preparing the two required springs and placing them in a placeholder, then inserting the springs from the placeholder into the switch. When a spring remained in the placeholder, the workers knew that they had forgotten to insert it and could correct the mistake effortlessly.

So why is mistaking proofing so important? Why is it a part of Lean Manufacturing?

The expected reason for Poka Yoke (Mistake Proofing) is that it reduces defects, reduces time on rework, and makes a process more effective. Eliminating waste is a beautiful thing.

It is interesting to understand the "How do we eliminate waste through mistake proofing" though. There are basically two ways of mistake proofing: (1) Prevention-based Poka Yoke and (2) Detection-based Poka Yoke.

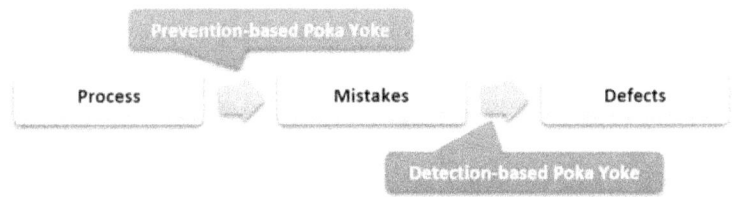

If you look at any system, the mistake happens as a part of that process. Processes either drift, steps are missed, or variability happens that cause a product not to satisfy specifications or requirements.

Each of these mistake conditions occur all the time and we need to have a multiple pronged approach as a solution to prevent them or detect them. That is why it is important to evaluate both methods.

The **Prevention-based** strategy tackles solving the issue before the mistake is made. Prevention-based Poka Yoke is the preferred method as it minimizes scrapped raw materials, wasted labor, lost time producing product, and the effort and time solving the problem and containing the issue. Prevention always saves the most money and makes the customer the most satisfied. The only time we say we don't want prevention is when you have to make the product before you can actually detect the issue (hopefully this is the exception) or the expense of prevention is prohibitive.

The **Detection-based** strategy focuses on being able to adequately find any mistakes before they go further down the process (adding more value to a wasted part) or worse, out to the customer (causing complaints or failures in the field). Detection involves knowing what the defects are and having adequate measuring systems to find those parts downstream from where the defects are made. There is also the probability that you scrap "good" parts in an effort to find all the "bad" parts.

The goal of these two strategies is to somehow either prevent the mistake from happening or be warned that a mistake was made.

Both of these strategies can rely on three types of Poka Yoke error proofing:
- Contact
- Fixed-value
- Motion-step

Contact methods are based on some type of sensing device which detects abnormalities in the product's shape or dimension and responds accordingly. Interference pins, notches with matching locator pins, limit switches and proximity switches are sometimes used to ensure that a part is positioned correctly before work occurs. Asymmetric parts with matching work fixtures can also alleviate incorrect positioning. If orientation is not critical, symmetrical designs can then be used to prevent defects.

Contact methods are useful in situations which encourage mistakes. Such situations involve rapid repetition, infrequent production, or environmental problems such as poor lighting, high or low heat, excess humidity, dust, noise, or anything which distracts a worker.

Fixed-value methods are used in processes where the same activity is repeated several times, such as tightening of bolts. This method frequently involves very simple techniques, such as methods that allow operators to easily track how often this activity has been performed.

An example of mistake proofing a "same activity" would be someone tightening down five bolts on a machine. Before passing the product on, the tightening process is performed a fixed number of times (five). A simple Poka Yoke device would incorporate the use of a wrench dipped in diluted paint. Since untightened bolts will not have paint on them, the operator can easily see if he or she has performed the process the required number of times.

A second example would be the use of pre-sorted, exact quantity, material used in a particular step. If the bolts were stored in containers of exactly five pieces, the operator would easily know when the step is complete once all bolts are utilized.

The **<u>Motion-step method</u>** is useful for processes requiring several different activities performed in sequence by a single operator. This is similar to the fixed-value situation in that the operator is responsible for multiple activities but instead of performing the same activity multiple times the operator performs different activities.

First, each step in the process is identified by the specific motions needed to complete it. Then devices are created to detect whether each motion is performed and then alert the operator when a step is skipped. An assembly process could utilize a device that senses when all required components are present at the start of the process for each unit. The devices could then detect when each component is removed from its dispenser. If a component is not removed, the sensing device alerts the assembler before he/she can move on to another unit.

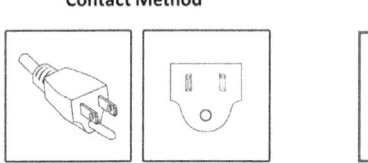
Contact Method

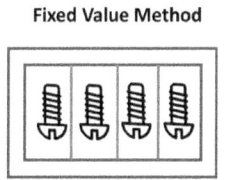
Fixed Value Method

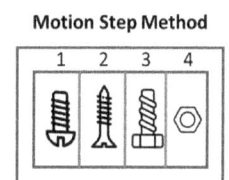
Motion Step Method

The examples above show basic Poka Yoke methods and how they work. The contact method example shows an electrical plug, in which there is only one way to connect them together. The Fixed Value example shows that there are four machine bolts required for the operation and if any bolt remains after the operation, something was missed. The Motion Step example placed each of the four parts in a sequence order, so each part is to be assembled in the appropriate order it was designated. Each method creates a scenario where it is harder for an issue to occur, thus avoiding mistakes - the literal definition of Poka Yoke.

Errors are inevitable in any manufacturing process, but if appropriate mistake proofing (or poka-yokes) are implemented, then mistakes can be caught quickly and prevented from resulting in defects. By eliminating defects at the source, the cost of mistakes within a company is reduced... and everyone is happy!

Poka Yoke Worksheet

Checklist and Tasks

- [ ] _____
- [ ] _____
- [ ] _____
- [ ] _____
- [ ] _____
- [ ] _____
- [ ] _____
- [ ] _____
- [ ] _____
- [ ] _____
- [ ] _____
- [ ] _____
- [ ] _____
- [ ] _____
- [ ] _____
- [ ] _____
- [ ] _____
- [ ] _____
- [ ] _____
- [ ] _____

Notes
- _____
- _____
- _____
- _____
- _____
- _____
- _____
- _____
- _____
- _____
- _____
- _____
- _____
- _____
- _____
- _____
- _____
- _____
- _____
- _____
- _____
- _____
- _____
- _____

Kanban - Lean's Inventory Tool

Yay... another Japanese word, isn't that awesome? "Kanban" (看板) translates directly into "visual signal" or "signboard." The most famous industrial engineer at Toyota, Taiichi Ohno, developed a system of cards that tracked materials and products and called it "Kanban." Now you know and the rest is history.

From a Lean perspective, kanbans are simple cards or locations that are used to track production throughout a plant. These cards or locations represent WIP (work in progress) stations where upper and lower limits are established to avoid excess inventory in any one location within a production line. Basically, the idea of a kanban is to have a scheduling system for manufacturing efficiency.

The critical aspect of a kanban is that it aligns with production consumption. The card or signal tells a supplier or material handler when material is needed (low level indicator), has too much material (high level indicator), and how much needs to be supplied (restocking quantity).

It should also be stated that these kanban locations also help to establish material availability for a "right on time" need basis.

So, here's an example of a kanban card. In the image below you can see a lot of critical information, including SKUs and descriptions. It is obvious that there is a minimum stock quantity of this part in this location and also a maximum limit of this stock quantity. It was also written what the current quantity is at this location, which is between the limits (this is a good thing).

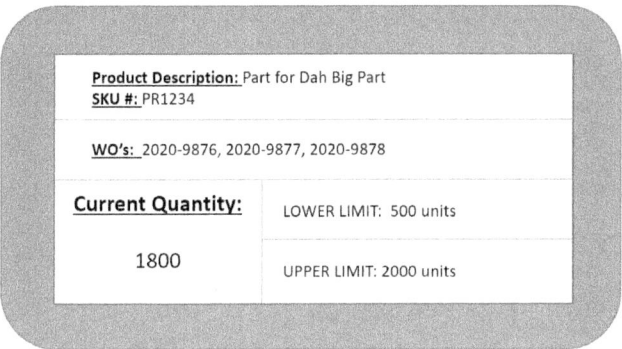

The lower limit makes sure there is material for the next WO or job to do. Having parts ready saves time with the material handling aspect of the process. No urgent call needed to the warehouse, no people standing around doing nothing because they're waiting for parts, and no leadership losing their marbles because there is lost production. Magic!

The most critical item to understand about the lower limit is what determines the lower limit. Typically, the lower limit is the quantity needed to start the next work order. You can change this lower limit based on a day or shift worth of work also, but that is where your team should analyze the situation and make the best decision.

The upper limit controls the urge for over inventory. This limit should be what makes sense for production to have enough material to smooth out disruptions in material flow. If someone is absent or you don't have many material handlers, you may set the upper limit to accommodate this gap.

Another simple use of visualizing workflow is with a general Kanban Board. In basic terms, you put needed activities into three areas: (1) Requested, (2) In Progress, and (3) Completed. In this way, you understand quickly where your team is bottlenecked at or where you need to move things along. Same Lean principle of improving the flow of product or work, but from a different process and level.

Just remember, the goal of a kanban is to control WIP, improve efficiencies, and make sure the process doesn't get out of control.

Setting up the system of a kanban should be analytical and practical. Use data and maintain simplicity. Keeping it simple at the beginning will help when you return to improve the kanban system later on because you understand the needs and constraints after you implement it.

Kanban Worksheet

Checklist and Tasks

☐ _____
☐ _____
☐ _____
☐ _____
☐ _____
☐ _____
☐ _____
☐ _____
☐ _____
☐ _____
☐ _____
☐ _____
☐ _____
☐ _____
☐ _____
☐ _____
☐ _____
☐ _____
☐ _____
☐ _____
☐ _____

Notes

OEE - Lean's Productivity Tool

Overall Equipment Effectiveness or OEE is the highest standard for measuring the productivity of a specific manufacturing process. OEE compiles three metrics into one result, therefore showing how close to perfect a process can be as it approaches the coveted result of 100%.

As just mentioned, the calculation of OEE involves three metrics: (1) Availability, (2) Performance, and (3) Quality or Yield. Each of these individual metrics is presented as a percentage. When you multiply them together, the resultant metric, OEE, is then also a percentage. Let's break each down individually.

Availability is the actual available operating time divided by the net available time, or simply stated the process "uptime." For example, if your production line is available 5 days a week for 24 hours each day, you have a net available time of 120 hours (5x24=120). If the actual operating time is only 20 hours a day for 3 days, the actual time is 60 hours. Taking the

60 hours of actual time and dividing it by the net available time of 120 hours, you have an availability of 50%.

$$\frac{Actual}{Net} = Availability \text{ or } \frac{60}{120} = 50\%$$

Performance is the speed efficiency of OEE, or the amount of produced parts divided by the standard of produced parts expected. If a process goes slower than expected, performance will be a fraction of the potential. If the process goes as fast as it can, performance will be at 100% of the standard. For example, if the theoretical best output of a process is 100 units an hour but the actual output is 80 units, the performance will be 80%.

$$\frac{Actual\ Output}{Theoretical\ Best\ Output} = Performance \text{ or } \frac{80}{100} = 80\%$$

Quality is the yield aspect of OEE or how many good units are produced per how many units produced. For example, a process produces 50 units per hour but only 45 units are good, it would have a yield of 90%.

$$\frac{Good\ Parts}{Total\ Parts\ Produced} = Quality \text{ or } \frac{45}{50} = 90\%$$

Note that when we have each aspect of the OEE equation, we can multiply the three percentages together to get an Overall Equipment Efficiency. For our example, we would multiply 50% by 80% by 90% for a total of 36%.

$$Availability \times Performance \times Quality = OEE$$
$$0.5 \times 0.8 \times 0.9 = 0.36 \text{ or } 36\% = OEE$$

So, the next question is "what is a good OEE result?"

The answer: It depends (Don't you love it when people say that?)

For general discussions, a 85% or better OEE would be excellent (in some operations, 85% OEE will be world class). If your OEE is between 75% and 85%, this is usually acceptable. If you are below 75%, this is considered poor OEE and the processes should be reviewed for improvement.

As you gather more data on the process and measure OEE over time, these limits will naturally change to a more appropriate target.

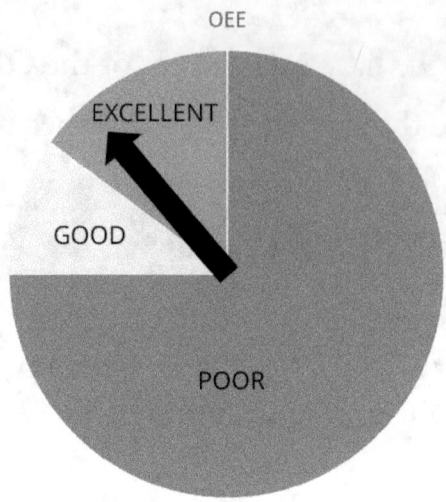

A great reason for using OEE in your processes is because it forces you to look at a goal and a result. If the result doesn't match the goal, you can analyze which category is responsible for the low OEE result and focus on improving that part of it.

In the calculation example above, an OEE of 36% is substandard. By looking at which category is hurting the result, it is obvious that it is the Availability portion of the OEE at 50%. Improving the time the process is running, thus improving your uptime, would be your next rational action for improvement.

By tracking changes in OEE over time, companies can measure the effectiveness of their improvement efforts and make further adjustments as needed. Overall, OEE is an essential tool for any organization looking to improve its production processes and increase efficiency.

OEE Worksheet

Checklist and Tasks

- [ ] _____
- [ ] _____
- [ ] _____
- [ ] _____
- [ ] _____
- [ ] _____
- [ ] _____
- [ ] _____
- [ ] _____
- [ ] _____
- [ ] _____
- [ ] _____
- [ ] _____
- [ ] _____
- [ ] _____
- [ ] _____
- [ ] _____
- [ ] _____
- [ ] _____
- [ ] _____
- [ ] _____
- [ ] _____

Notes
-
-
-
-
-
-
-
-
-
-
-
-
-
-
-
-
-
-
-
-
-
-
-
-

Lean's Root Cause Analysis Tools

There are a thousand different ways to analyze a problem. When you have a strategy on finding out the primary reason a problem exists, this is called Root Cause Analysis. I think the most detailed root cause analysis is the Six Sigma approach but there are simpler tools that one can use to find the root cause of a problem. Two tools will be discussed: (1) 5 Why's, and (2) the Fishbone diagram.

Root Cause Analysis: 5 Why's

5 Why's is a simple technique where you keep asking "why" until you arrive at a foundational cause for a problem. This method is not suggested for medium to difficult problems but rather simpler or moderate problems.

The 5 Why's start by defining what the problem is. This is done with an Upper Level box (see Step 1 in image below).

**Step 1:
Define the Problem**

**Step 2:
Ask general questions about the issue**

Defining the problem will generate several additional questions about the problem that need addressing, which is our Step 2. These questions are a mental exercise to categorize your thoughts around what creates the problem. Many of the questions may stay unanswered (saved for later) but are important to have on paper.

The third step is to ask what are the potential problem areas where the problem could develop (next level box). Once you have a few Problem Area's defined (as in image below), you begin asking "why does this occur?" for each of the problem areas.

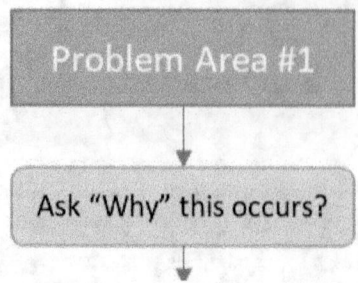

As you continue to ask "Why," you will eventually get to a point where you can establish a countermeasure to prevent the issue from happening. Once all problem areas are counter measured, the process is monitored to look for improvement. If no improvement is noticed, additional problem areas could be added or additional "why's" could be asked until root cause is found.

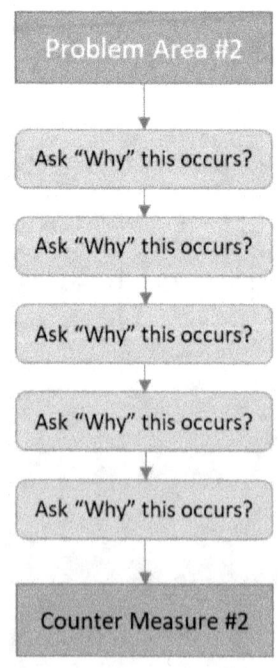

Again, the idea of asking "Why?" so many times is to drill to the true cause of the problem. Many times our first response or initial correction will only temporarily remedy the problem or will only satisfy the superficial elements of the problem. Understanding the core issue of the problem requires diligent investigation that peels away all the outer layers thereby revealing the inner, "true cause" of the problem. Once you see the true cause, the counter measure will more accurately correct or mitigate the problem.

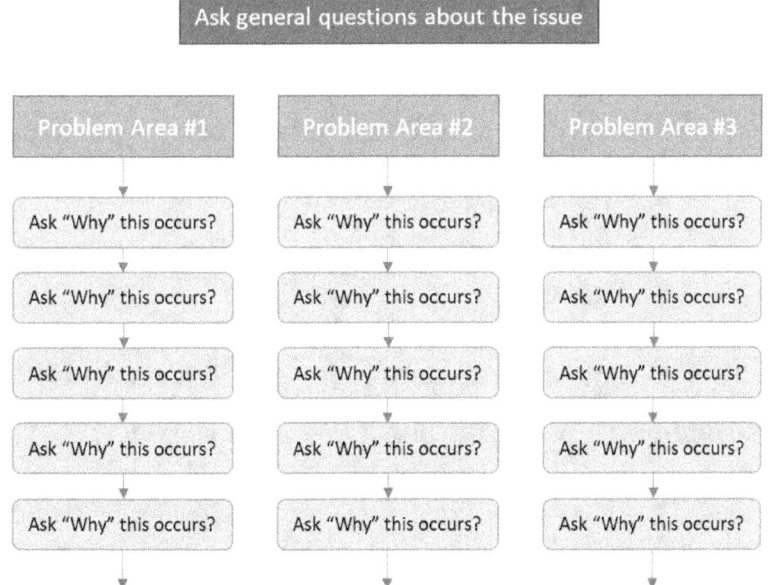

Root Cause Analysis: Fishbone Diagram

The **Fishbone Diagram** is another root cause investigation tool. This method is more visual than the 5 Why's method and is used for minor to middle range issue complexity. The reason why fishbone diagrams can solve more complicated issues is because of the branching nature of the diagram and how it displays the data in a *Cause and Effect* manner. The visual display of the root cause analysis actually resembles the look of a fishbone, with a tad dose of imagination.

When you utilize a fishbone diagram, you start in the same way as the 5 Why's method, by stating what the problem or defect is.

The ***Problem*** becomes the "head" of the fish, the centerpoint of the Fishbone Diagram. The head could also be represented as a "Defect," if this makes analyzing the factors easier.

The "bone" structure is composed of ***Critical Areas of Cause***, being (1) Measurement, (2) Materials, (3) Personnel, (4) Environment, (5) Methods, and (6) Machines. These Six Critical Areas help segment the potential causes into architectural bones that need further exploration.

These areas form the basic structure of the fishbone, as seen below. These "Bones" are intended to encompass all possible causes that create or help create the problem under investigation.

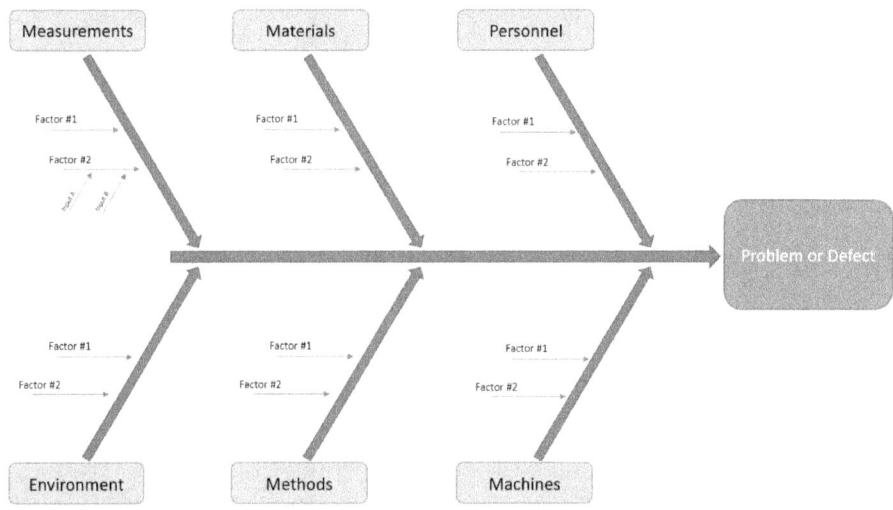

Within each critical area are **Factors** that influence that respective critical area, that could then influence or create the problem or defect being investigated.

Within each factor, there are **Inputs** that influence the factor it is listed under. It is very probable that there are several inputs for every factor and several factors for every critical area. This can be seen in this image.

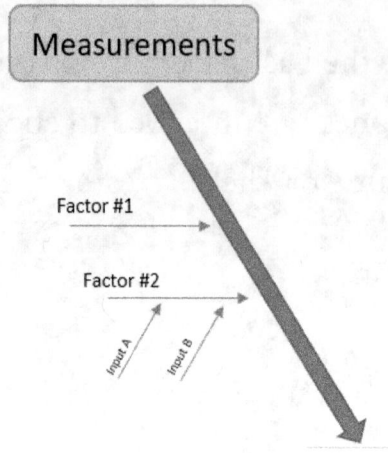

An example of a fishbone critical area is shown below. Let's say the problem under investigation is "My Motorcycle Doesn't Work." You would take each critical area and list every factor that fits under that specific area.

For the example of a motorcycle not working, under "Materials," you could list two factors being "Oil" and another "Fuel." One would then list what inputs into these factors could cause the problem to occur. For the "Oil" factor, one input could be "Oil is Missing" and another input could be "Wrong Oil Used." For the second factor "Fuel," one input could be "Fuel Missing" while another input could be "Fuel Contaminated."

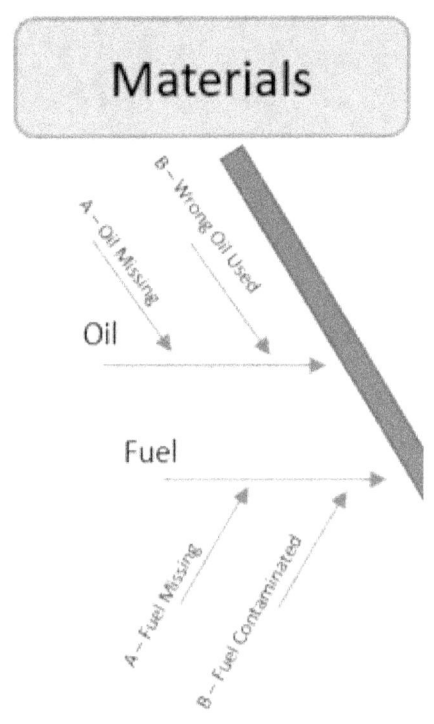

One could continue listing factors and inputs until all possible combinations are listed that influence or create the problem under that critical area. You would continue under each critical area until all factors and inputs are listed.

Once the fishbone diagram is complete, the next step is to circle the most likely inputs to test. You should not circle more than a few (three to five) so that you can investigate and test to see if those inputs truly influence or create the problem. Repeating this cycle may be necessary to completely correct the defect and definitely identify the root cause.

Fishbone diagrams are very useful but aren't perfect. The simpler the process, the simpler the fishbone diagram. The reverse is also true. The more complicated the process, the more complicated the fishbone diagram becomes. This is the advantage and disadvantage of a fishbone, it can be simple and therefore clean and easy to analyze or complicated and timely and difficult to figure out.

Remember, the objective of the fishbone is to understand the possible inputs ("Causes") that could contribute or influence to the problem/defect ("Effect") and thereby finding the "true" root cause to the problem. The closure occurs when the problem is remedied and the defect disappears.

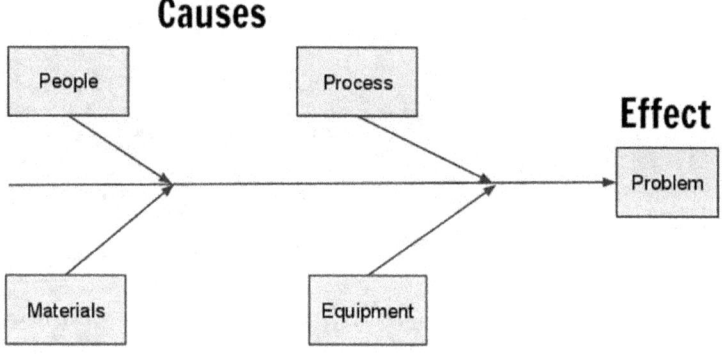

Root Cause Analysis Worksheet

Checklist and Tasks

☐ _____
☐ _____
☐ _____
☐ _____
☐ _____
☐ _____
☐ _____
☐ _____
☐ _____
☐ _____
☐ _____
☐ _____
☐ _____
☐ _____
☐ _____
☐ _____
☐ _____
☐ _____
☐ _____
☐ _____
☐ _____

Notes

- _____
- _____
- _____
- _____
- _____
- _____
- _____
- _____
- _____
- _____
- _____
- _____
- _____
- _____
- _____
- _____
- _____
- _____
- _____
- _____
- _____
- _____
- _____

Step Seven: Kaizen Event

Japanese is an interesting language. I have studied it for years and still am chipping away at it daily. Words typically are a combination of different words or Kanji to make a new word. We do this all the time in English - such as bookstore, downtown, and tabletop. "Kaizen (改善)" is no different and also a combination of two words, "Kai (改)" meaning "change" and "Zen (善)" meaning "good." A "good change" in Japanese translates into "improvement" in English. So a Kaizen event is literally an improvement event.

With this definition in mind, what we are trying to accomplish with a Kaizen event is an improvement to a process within a short period of time. No magic, just smart, hard work.

A Kaizen event is the center of the Lean process, as shown in the Lean Manufacturing diagram. During a Kaizen event, a team of employees works together to identify areas for improvement and develop solutions to address them. The team uses data analysis and information from the Value Stream map to identify inefficiencies and waste in the current process (Opportunity Bursts). They then brainstorm ideas for how to eliminate these inefficiencies and implement changes that will lead to improved performance.

With a team in place and a scope defined, all you have to do is start an improvement activity, which in Lean terms is a Kaizen event.

As stated previously, you want to do a project large enough to take a few days but typically no longer than a week so activities and action items don't linger any longer than necessary. If it will only take a day to do, just do it without the structure of an event - this is common sense and the Lean mentality at work. If it takes longer than a week, you probably have multiple Kaizen events that are needed or your scope is too large.

Kaizen events typically follow a simple project management format. The Kaizen starts with a planning stage, then an implement or workshop stage, and then a follow-up or close out stage. As basic as the process of a Kaizen is, let's still go through each stage and understand what is needed and completed.

The **Planning Stage** is probably the most overlooked part of the Kaizen Event. It is overlooked because individuals want to solve the problem so much that they lack the patience and maturity to carefully plan and strategize what is needed for the Kaizen to be successful. Recall what is needed in the planning stage is:

- <u>The project scope</u> - the scope should be identified by now based simply on wanting a Kaizen event but should be reviewed with the project team and management to confirm that the focus area and the needed results are accurate.

- <u>The project team</u> - This team should be cross functional and should have some ownership of the success. The team should also be able to contribute data or effort into the improvement activities in the execution or workshop stage.
- <u>Kaizen goals and objectives</u> - The required results and benefits should be documented and agreed upon. Specific goals and objectives should be dissected into appropriate actions and activities that will measure success and progress.
- <u>Kaizen Agenda</u> - To keep the team motivated and on track, an agenda can be helpful to communicate timing and next steps so that the team can continue to be in harmony with each member and activity.

The **Implementation Phase** is the action phase of the Kaizen event. Now that you have a scope, a team, goals, and an agenda, your focus is on executing the plan. The stages of this phase are:

- <u>Baseline Data</u> - Conducting a thorough analysis of the current process or system (or reviewing your VSM) will help answer foundational questions of how effective and efficient the process and system are.

- <u>Brainstorming and Challenging Status</u> - Understanding what root cause tools or Lean tools to help solve the problem and challenging where are the most impactful improvement areas.
- <u>Experimenting</u> - Testing out the assumptions of the improvements and answering early questions to streamline next decisions and directions.
- <u>Implementation</u> - Implement all changes and improvements to the process or system.

To finish off the Kaizen Event, we go into the **Follow-Up Phase**. This is another phase that gets ignored too often. A team needs to make sure that the gains will be sustained and that results meet the expectations of the scope. This stage is divided into these parts:

- <u>Results</u> - Measuring the success of the event through data analysis and feedback from the stakeholders.
- <u>Celebration</u> - Celebrating the successes and identifying areas for future improvements.
- <u>Sustainment</u> - Implementing long term plans to sustain the changes made during the event.

An example of a Kaizen event happened recently. We had a manufacturing line that needed to be on a single shift instead of multiple shifts. The idea was that multiple shifts required a lot more support staff and communication to produce the required weekly output for the market than that of a single shift.

A team of cross functional members were assembled (production / planning / operators / engineering / maintenance / quality) on a certain Tuesday morning. The team was assembled after getting set for the day's work in a conference room in the facility. Getting the team together, away from their desks, allowed them to be focused on the Kaizen event.

- First was a 45 minute training review of key Lean tools and theory to ground them in the right mentality and to help remind them of what Lean processes to use.
- Next was a head first dive into the Value Stream Map of what the process and current state was. It was drafted in a conference room and then verified by going to where the operations are performed and verifying all steps, cycle times, and inventory levels.
- Once the Value Stream was complete, target Kaizen Bursts or Opportunities were circled and analyzed for improvement projections.
- The following days were spent doing 5S, Visual Management, and other improvement activities.
- The Kaizen Event was closed at the end of the week by summarizing the accomplishments and presenting them

to the management team (who rewarded the team for their efforts).

Efficiency of your time and getting the improvements implemented quickly is the goal of the Kaizen event. The more complicated and extensive a project, the more time it will take and the more likely you won't get it accomplished in a reasonable amount of time.

Speed for improvement is a tenet of a good Lean program (no Zombies allowed though).

The goal of a Kaizen event is not just to make one-time improvements, but rather to establish a culture of continuous improvement within the organization. By empowering employees at all levels of the organization to identify problems and develop solutions, Kaizen events can help drive innovation and increase productivity over time.

Action Items for Step Seven:

- Start your Kaizen with the planning phase by selecting a cross-functional team and reviewing the project scope.
- Identify your objectives for the Kaizen event by clearly defining what specific improvements are you aiming for.
- Make sure the objectives are measurable and achievable within the timeframe of the event.
- Provide any necessary training to team members on the Kaizen methodology, problem-solving techniques, and any specific tools or methodologies they'll be using during the event.
- Gather relevant data related to the process being targeted for improvement or review your VSM. This might include cycle times, defect rates, customer feedback, etc. Ensure data accuracy and reliability.
- Conduct brainstorming sessions with the team to generate ideas for improvement. Encourage creativity and innovation. Use techniques like mind mapping or affinity diagrams to organize ideas.
- Prioritize the generated ideas based on their potential impact, feasibility, and alignment with the event objectives.

- Select the most promising improvement opportunities to focus on during the event.
- Develop a detailed plan outlining how each improvement idea will be implemented.
- Assign responsibilities and establish timelines for implementation.
- Continuously monitor the implemented changes and measure their impact on key performance indicators (KPIs).
- Collect feedback from employees and stakeholders to identify further areas for improvement.
- Document the new standard operating procedures or best practices resulting from the Kaizen event. Ensure that these are communicated and enforced throughout the organization.
- Celebrate the success of the Kaizen event and recognize the contributions of team members. Reinforce a culture of continuous improvement within the organization.
- Schedule follow-up meetings or reviews to track the long-term impact of the improvements and identify additional opportunities for optimization.

Step Seven Worksheet

Kaizen Checklist and Tasks

- [ ] _____
- [ ] _____
- [ ] _____
- [ ] _____
- [ ] _____
- [ ] _____
- [ ] _____
- [ ] _____
- [ ] _____
- [ ] _____
- [ ] _____
- [ ] _____
- [ ] _____
- [ ] _____
- [ ] _____
- [ ] _____
- [ ] _____
- [ ] _____
- [ ] _____
- [ ] _____

Notes

Conclusion

The path through Lean manufacturing principles has been a marvelous journey for those who start the road of continuous improvement. From its inception on the factory floors of Toyota to its widespread adoption across industries worldwide, the core tenets of Lean - waste reduction, continuous improvement, and customer focus - have proven transformative.

Throughout this book, we've explored the fundamental concepts of lean manufacturing, from value stream mapping, to kanban systems, to mistake-proofing techniques. Each concept, when implemented with dedication and effort, has the potential to streamline processes, enhance quality, and boost efficiency.

However, beyond its tangible benefits lies a deeper purpose. Lean manufacturing is not merely a set of tools and methodologies; it's a mindset, a culture of relentless pursuit of perfection. Lean fosters collaboration, empowers employees, and creates a spirit of innovation.

What has been unbelievable over the many years of my career and will be in the future of our rapidly evolving industrial landscape, Lean manufacturing has remained as relevant as ever. In an era defined by volatility, uncertainty, complexity, and ambiguity, Lean principles offer a compass to navigate challenges and seize opportunities. Whether in traditional manufacturing sectors or emerging fields like healthcare and software development, the principles of Lean can catalyze transformation and drive sustainable growth.

Most important among the principles of Lean manufacturing is who it should matter to most. As we continue to refine our processes and optimize our systems, let us remain steadfast in our commitment to delivering value to customers through the relentless pursuit of excellence.

In closing, let this book serve as a guide and inspiration on your own Lean journey. May you embrace the principles of Lean manufacturing not as mere strategies or tools, but as a philosophy that transcends boundaries and unlocks the true potential of our own creativity. Together, we can build efficiency, effectiveness, and excellence wherever in the world we find ourselves. We, all together, can take processes and products from mediocre to good and then to great... Maybe even to a point beyond what we thought possible.

Let's refine to the point of excellence!

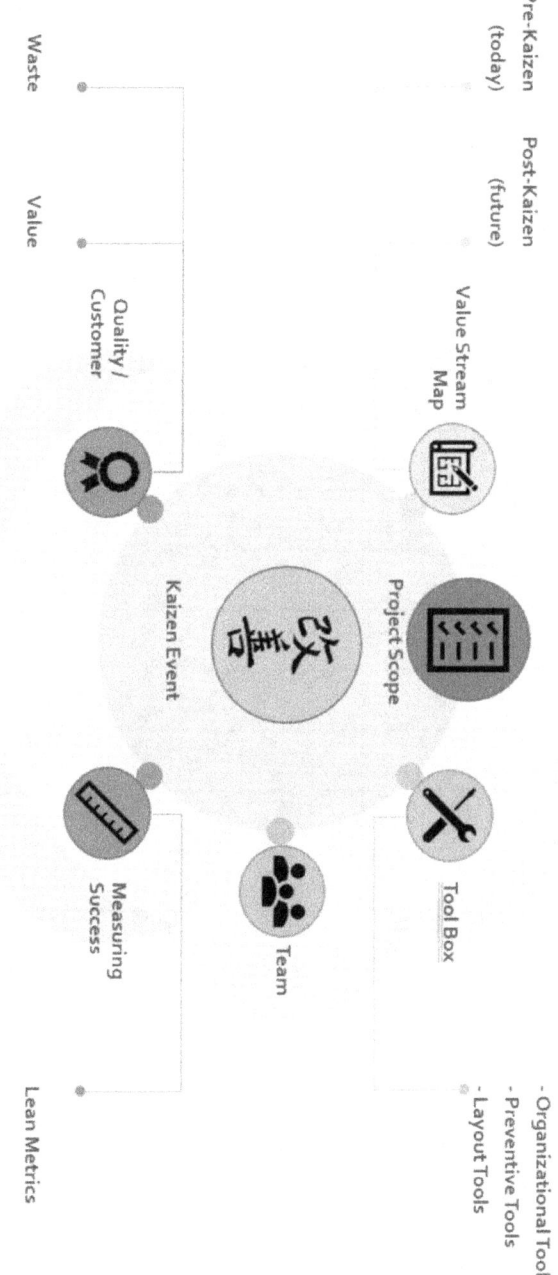

Notes

Notes

-
-
-
-
-
-
-
-
-
-
-
-
-
-
-
-
-
-
-
-
-
-
-
-
-

Notes

Author Biography

Richard Jepson is a degreed Biological and Chemical Engineer with over two decades of experience in the Medical Device manufacturing industry. Having worked in some of the finest manufacturing arenas around the world and on several billion-dollar products, Lean Manufacturing has been an integral part of Richard's career. Teaching the fundamental principles of continuous improvement, such as Lean Manufacturing, has been and continues to be one of his greatest passions and interests.